Why do people Smoke?

Jillian Powell

HODDER
Wayland

an imprint of Hodder Children's Books

© 2000 White-Thomson Publishing Ltd

Produced for Hodder Wayland by
White-Thomson Publishing Ltd
2/3 St Andrew's Place
Lewes
BN7 1UP
East Sussex

Series concept: Alex Woolf
Series editor: Liz Gogerly
Book editor: Cath Senker
Consultant: John Bennett, Health Education
        Advisor, Birmingham
Picture research: Gina Brown – Glass Onion
        Pictures
Cover Design: Hodder Children's Books
Inside Design: Stonecastle Graphics Ltd
Proofreader: Sarah Doughty

First published in Great Britain in 2000
by Hodder Wayland, an imprint of
Hodder Children's Books
This paperback edition published in 2001

The right of Jillian Powell to be identified as the
author has been asserted by her in accordance
with the Copyright, Designs and Patents Act 1988.

A Catalogue record for this book is available from
the British Library.

ISBN 0 7502 2765 6

Printed and bound in Italy by G. Canale & C.S.p.A.

Hodder Children's Books
A division of Hodder Headline Limited
338 Euston Road
London
NW1 3BH

Picture acknowledgements
The publisher would like to thank the following
for their kind permission to use their pictures:
British Museum 4 (below); Mark Douet cover; Eye
Ubiquitous (Bennett Dean) 6, (John Dakers) 8,
(David Cumming) 30 (above), (K. Wilton) 33, (Gary
Trotter) 35, (Paul Seheult) 42 (below); Sally
Greenhill 42 (above); HWPL (Angela Hampton)
contents page (below), 4 (above), 7, 9, (Zak
Waters) 11 (below),12, (APM Studios) 13, (Angus
Blackburn) 19, 22, 23, 27, (Rupert Horrox) 29,
(Angela Hampton) 31, 39, 40 (both), 44; Impact
(Simon Shepheard) 21, (Andy Johnstone) 28,
Caroline Penn 32 (above), (Ben Edwards) 38; James
Davis Travel Photography 17 (below); Mary Evans
Picture Library 5; National Film Archive 10; Panos
Pictures (Giacomo Pirozzi) contents page (above),
11 (above); Quadrant Picture Library 36; Science
Photo Library (Art Siegel/Custom Medical Stock
Photo 16, (Damien Lovegrove) 17 (above), (Colin
Cuthbert) 25, (James Stevenson) 26 (below),
(Neil Bromhall) 32 (below); Skjold 24; South
American Pictures (Tony Morrison) 14, (Rolando
Pujol) 34; Roger Vlitos 15, 20, 26 (above), 30
(below), 37, 41; White-Thomson Publishing Ltd
title page, 18, 43, 45.

Cover picture: a cigarette in an ashtray

IMPORTANT NOTE: Models have been used for all
the photos in this book.

Contents

1. How smoking became popular

How was smoking discovered?

Did you know that tobacco was used thousands of years ago? The leaves of the tobacco plant were being chewed or smoked long before people understood what tobacco contained or what it did to their health.

Tobacco plants were growing in the Americas as early as 6000 BC. Native Americans smoked peace-pipes of tobacco in religious ceremonies and used it to dress wounds. Chewing tobacco was believed to cure toothache. The Mayan people of Central America smoked tobacco from around AD 500. In 1492, Native Americans gave dried tobacco leaves to the explorer, Christopher Columbus, as a gift. Soon after, tobacco was being grown all over Europe. Some doctors believed that tobacco could cure anything from bad breath to cancer.

▲ *Native Americans believed that smoking tobacco could cure everything from toothache to earache. Sometimes, they mixed tobacco leaves with other plants to change the flavour.*

▶ *Native American pipes were works of art. Each man kept his own special pipe, although it was often passed round a group to be smoked.*

By the 1600s, tobacco had become so popular in Europe that it was often used as money. During the 1700s, smoking fell out of fashion as taking tobacco in the form of snuff became popular with men. But in the 1800s, the first cigarette factories opened, and cigarettes were produced in large numbers.

▼ *This man is sniffing powdered tobacco, called snuff. In the 18th century, snuff took over in Europe as the fashionable way to take tobacco.*

The first health warnings came after pure nicotine was discovered in 1826. In the USA, Samuel Green from New England stated that tobacco was a poison that could kill people.

Yet cigarettes were handed out to soldiers during the First World War (1914–18). Also, many women began to smoke, especially as more of them went out to work. By the 1920s and '30s, smoking had become fashionable. But during the 1950s, medical reports began to appear linking smoking with lung cancer.

FACT:
People did not really understand that smoking could cause deadly diseases until quite recently. In the 1950s, the first major studies in Britain and the USA linked smoking with lung cancer.

Tobacco

Cigarettes, cigars and pipes all contain tobacco, made from the leaves of the tobacco plant. To make cigarettes, the leaves are dried, shredded and mixed with chemicals to keep them moist, then rolled in paper. As the tobacco burns, the smoke is breathed into the body.

◀ *This boy in Yunnan province, China is holding tobacco leaves that have been dried in the sun.*

The Native American peoples found that chewing or smoking tobacco could calm their nerves and make them feel relaxed. This is because of the drug nicotine, which is in the tobacco leaves. When people smoke or chew tobacco, nicotine gets into their bloodstream. The drug quickly reaches the smoker's brain and begins to make them feel good.

"

'*Nicotiana tabacum* – the tobacco plant, the most dangerous plant on the planet, currently killing around 4 million people annually.'
GASP Smoke-free Solutions

"

case study · case study · case study ·

Marion has been a smoker nearly all her life. She cannot imagine getting through the day without her cigarettes. She keeps them by her bed so she can light up when she wakes in the morning. Most days, she smokes about forty cigarettes.

Marion knows that her cough is caused by smoking, and last year she had to go into hospital because of heart trouble. The doctors told her she was damaging her health and should give up her cigarettes and fried breakfasts.

Marion knows her health is bad, but she is not willing to give up the things she enjoys most. Her work in the call centre is really boring, and she has lived on her own since getting divorced. She feels she needs her cigarettes just to get through life. Marion tells her doctor she will try to quit smoking, but secretly she feels you have to die of something, and it might as well be something you enjoy.

▼ *Marion really enjoys her cigarettes and is not willing to give them up.*

Smoking – a global habit

Today, about a third of all adults worldwide – 1.1 billion people – are smokers. In the USA, approximately 50 million people are smokers. In the developed world, the number of smokers has been falling because more is known about the health risks, and there are now more anti-smoking laws. But in countries such as China, Russia and Poland, the number of smokers is increasing, especially among young people. China is now the world's largest producer and consumer of tobacco. The number of cigarettes smoked per person in the population more than doubled between 1965 and 1990. Eastern Europe is also a growing market. Russia is now the third largest market for tobacco consumption, after China and the USA.

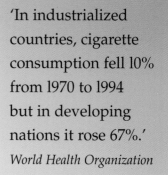

'In industrialized countries, cigarette consumption fell 10% from 1970 to 1994 but in developing nations it rose 67%.'
World Health Organization

As smoking begins in a country, it follows this pattern:
♦ the men take it up first
♦ the number of men smoking rises rapidly, then falls
♦ boys begin to smoke, following the same pattern as the men
♦ women start smoking
♦ finally, girls take up the habit.

▶ *Young women in Tokyo, Japan. In Japan, the number of young women smokers rose by more than 5 per cent between 1970 and 1990.*

Worldwide, poor and unemployed people are most likely to become regular smokers. Tobacco production and sales add to the problems of poverty and disease in the developing world. Smokers who are poor may choose between buying cigarettes and food. In Bangladesh, if a man smokes just five cigarettes a day, his children may not be getting enough food to eat.

Tobacco also has an environmental cost. Many developing countries grow tobacco for export but do not grow enough food crops to feed their own people. Tobacco plants need lots of chemical fertilizers, which can make the land unfit for growing food.

Thousands of hectares of forest are cut down to provide firewood to dry the tobacco leaves. One tree is cut down every fortnight for each person who smokes twenty cigarettes a day.

> '**Tobacco growing is a key element of the economy in many developing countries in Africa and South America.**'
> *The Tobacco Manufacturers' Association*

▶ *This man in India is smoking through a water-pipe called a hookah.*

2. Becoming a smoker

Why do people start smoking?

Do any of your family or friends smoke? Do you know how old they were when they started smoking? People start smoking for different reasons. Most people who are regular smokers start smoking when they are in their early teens, or even younger.

Sometimes, people start smoking because they want to find out what it is like. Their first cigarette may make them feel sick or dizzy, but they see other people enjoying cigarettes and they want to get the same feeling. After a while, they get used to smoking.

Many people think smoking looks cool, or grown-up. It first had this image in the 1930s. All the famous film stars smoked, and their fans wanted to look like them. Films can make smoking look glamorous. Seeing film or rock stars smoking makes some fans want to do so too, just as they want to dress like them or talk like them. Smoking is part of the image.

▲ Film stars like Rita Hayworth made smoking look glamorous to our grandparents and great-grandparents.

‘Every sleeping and waking hour from billboards, TV screens, movies, radios and now the Internet, the tobacco industry beckons our children.’
World Health Organization Tobacco-Free Initiative

Some people start smoking to try to impress boyfriends or girlfriends or to fit in with a crowd. They are afraid they will be left out if they say they don't want to smoke. Friends can encourage people to smoke. If they are smokers, they want their mates to be like them, so they can smoke together and lend each other cigarettes. If your family or friends smoke, it can feel like the natural thing to do. Surveys show that children whose family or friends smoke are much more likely to become regular smokers themselves.

▲ *This young Rwandan boy lives on the streets. He has become a smoker and so now he has to beg for money for cigarettes as well as for food.*

▶ *When friends offer cigarettes, it can be hard to refuse. But saying 'no' shows that you know your own mind, and aren't afraid to stand your ground.*

11

Smoking as a comfort

Sometimes, people start to smoke when they are feeling worried or under stress. They might have changed schools or jobs, or be taking important exams. They may have problems at home that no one seems to understand. Perhaps they feel they need something to help them get by, so they turn to cigarettes. Smoking can feel comforting and help people to concentrate or to relax.

Child smokers
Percentage of regular smoking (at least one cigarette per week) 1996

Source: ONS Survey among secondary schoolchildren, quoted in The Guardian, 9 February, 2000

▲ *This graph shows that one-third of 15-year-old girls in the UK smoked in 1996.*

▲ *Going to school can be stressful, especially if you have exams coming up.*

FACTS:
UK surveys show that many people smoke their first cigarette between the ages of 9 and 12.
(Source: Health Education Authority, UK)
In the USA, 60% of smokers start smoking before they are 14 - and 90% before they are 21.
90% of teenagers who smoke a few cigarettes will become regular smokers.

case study · case study · case study ·

Leanne started smoking when she was thirteen, after her grandmother Ellen died. Leanne and her grandmother had been really close. Leanne sometimes felt she was the only person who understood her. Ellen had been a heavy smoker. When she was sixty, she became ill with lung cancer. She was ill for about a year before she died. Everyone said she was her own worst enemy because she wouldn't give up smoking.

After her grandmother died, Leanne had a rough time at school. She didn't have any close friends and she missed her grandmother a lot. When she started smoking, it felt as if she was somehow getting closer to her. Everyone had been cross with Leanne too, as they had been with Ellen. The first time Leanne's mum saw her smoking she was really shocked. She said, 'You're going the same way as your grandmother.'

'I started smoking around the time I changed schools. It was hard to make new friends at first, and everything was strange. Then I got in with a new crowd. They all seemed to smoke, so I did too. It makes you feel like you belong.'

Dan, aged 14

▶ *Every day of every year, families lose loved ones to smoking-related diseases. Smoking is the biggest cause of lung cancer.*

A way of rebelling

Smoking can be a way of rebelling against teachers or parents. Most people now know that smoking can harm their health. But smoking can be like wearing a badge that says 'I am old enough to decide for myself. If I want to smoke, I will. If I want to risk my health, I can, because it is my body.'

Some people point out that the health warnings on packets of cigarettes may even encourage some people to smoke. Smokers like to feel they can take risks and are not scared of the warnings. Taking risks may even be a way of proving that they feel grown-up and in control. This is why one US manufacturer made cigarettes with the brand name 'Death'.

> 'In the young smoker's mind, a cigarette falls into the same category as wine, beer, shaving, wearing a bra…
> a declaration of independence and striving for self-identity.'
> *Extract from a marketing report for the tobacco industry*

◀ *These children in Brazil are hanging out with teenagers, which can encourage them to start smoking early.*

> 'They are always warning us about something, aren't they? Don't eat this, don't do that. You risk your life every time you cross the road, don't you?'
>
> *Nina, aged 15*

◀ *Young people may think it is cool to smoke.*

What does smoking say about you?

♦ This is my body, OK?
♦ I can take risks
♦ I am a bit of a daredevil
♦ I can handle this
or
♦ I don't mind if my breath and clothes smell of smoke
♦ I don't mind spending my money on tobacco
♦ I don't mind nicotine being in control of me
♦ I can cope with illness and disease

FACT:
In some Latin American cities, 50% of teenagers smoke. The younger people are when they first start to smoke, the higher their risk of getting lung cancer and other diseases.
(Source: Health Education Authority)

3. 'I need a cigarette'

Why is smoking addictive?

Have you ever heard a smoker say 'I need a cigarette'? What do you think makes them feel this need? Their body is telling them to smoke because it has become addicted to nicotine.

Nicotine can calm someone down when they are feeling worried or upset, or it can make them feel lively and in control when they have been feeling tired or bored. It works quickly, so the smoker feels better almost immediately. The nicotine passes into tiny tubes in the lungs and then into the bloodstream. It reaches the brain in about seven seconds. Once a person has started smoking, their body gets used to nicotine and starts to need it. This is called addiction.

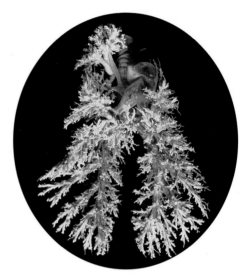

▲ A model of the human lungs. The tiny tubes shown here in pink and white are called bronchioles. They carry nicotine into a smoker's bloodstream.

FACT:
Nicotine is measured in milligrams per cigarette: the amount of nicotine ranges from less than 0.1 mg per cigarette to just over 1.0 mg. The drug is named after Jean Nicot, the courtier who started the fashion for smoking at the French royal court in the 16th century.

FACT:
Nicotine replacement products such as nicotine gum and skin patches can help smokers give up. They give low doses of nicotine without the other poisonous chemicals in tobacco smoke. These products are safer and less addictive than cigarettes, and help quitters get through the craving for nicotine.

▲ *This woman is using a nicotine inhaler. It gives a low dose of nicotine.*

◀ *This young boy in Indonesia feels proud that he is grown-up enough to smoke.*

Nicotine – as addictive as heroin

Soon after a cigarette has been smoked, the level of nicotine in a smoker's blood drops quickly. This can happen even faster if they are eating, or feeling worried or nervous. They start to feel jumpy and can't relax. Soon, they need to smoke another cigarette to feel better again.

Nicotine is as addictive as heroin. As a smoker's body gets used to nicotine, they need to smoke more often. Smokers may start to feel the need to smoke every twenty to forty-five minutes to keep up the level of nicotine in their blood. Some people become chain-smokers, smoking up to sixty cigarettes a day.

'A cigarette is a carefully crafted product that delivers just the right amount of nicotine to keep its user addicted for life before killing the person.'
Dr Gro Harlem Brundtland, Director General of the World Health Organization

◀ *Some people chain-smoke – lighting one cigarette from another they are already smoking.*

Rajeema has smoked for years. She works in a local government office which has a no-smoking policy. When she is at work, Rajeema has to go and stand outside the building to have a cigarette. Some of her workmates come too and they enjoy a chat and a smoke.

Rajeema also smokes when she is out with her friends. Smoking stops her from feeling so shy when she meets someone new. People are always handing round cigarettes and smoking makes Rajeema feel she is part of the crowd.

Rajeema's friend Jamila would like to give up because she wants to save money to get married next year, but it's hard saying no all the time. Sometimes, the blokes make fun of Jamila because she doesn't want to smoke and won't drink because she is driving. Rajeema feels sorry for Jamila, but Jamila is determined to give up.

▲ *Many smokers use coffee and lunch breaks to have a cigarette. In cities, they can often be seen smoking outside offices that have no-smoking policies.*

Some people reach for a cigarette when they first wake up in the morning. Others smoke with a cup of coffee or after a meal. It is common for people to smoke when they are doing something stressful, such as working or driving. Cigarettes can also help people feel relaxed at parties, or when they meet new people for the first time.

4. The health risks of smoking

What are the risks of smoking?

How would you rate the health risks of smoking? Some people say that everything in life is a risk, and you have to die of something. But there are some risks you can avoid, such as smoking. It is something we can choose not to do, like running across a busy motorway.

There are over 4,000 chemicals and gases in the smoke from a burning cigarette. Many of them are poisonous. When a smoker inhales, these pass into the body.
They include:
♦ Carbon monoxide, which is a gas found in car exhaust fumes
♦ Nicotine
♦ Sticky black tar
♦ Traces of pesticides
♦ Poisonous metals such as arsenic, and hydrogen cyanide, a poisonous liquid.

When a cigarette is smoked, smoke passes along the bronchial tubes leading to the lungs. These tubes are lined with tiny hairs that keep dirt and germs out of the lungs. Tobacco smoke damages the hairs so the bronchial tubes may become blocked, and cannot keep out germs so well.

▲ *As this cigarette burns, thousands of poisonous chemicals are released. At least 40 are believed to cause cancer.*

Nicotine makes the heart beat faster and raises the blood pressure, putting extra strain on the smoker's heart. Carbon monoxide makes it harder for the blood to carry oxygen round the body. Carbon monoxide, along with nicotine, can thicken the blood, which can lead to heart disease.

Soot and tar stick to the lungs and the bronchial tubes. This can cause coughs and breathing problems, and lead to lung diseases including lung cancer, emphysema and bronchitis.

▼ *A poster showing the dangers of tar. Light cigarettes have less tar and nicotine. But smokers may inhale them more deeply and take in the same amount of tar and nicotine as from normal cigarettes.*

FACTS:
Smoking causes
90% of deaths
from lung cancer
worldwide.
Tobacco use is
estimated to
cause 20% of all
deaths worldwide.
Someone dies
every 8 seconds
from a smoking-
related disease.
(Source: World
Health Organization)

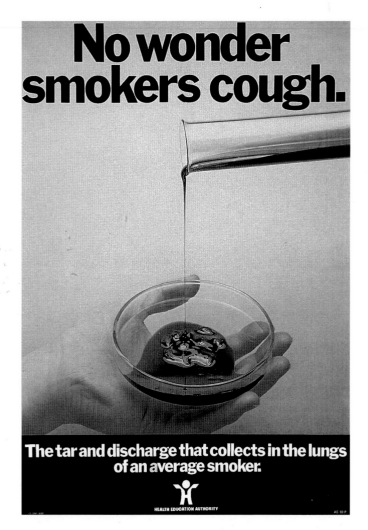

No wonder smokers cough.

The tar and discharge that collects in the lungs of an average smoker.

HEALTH EDUCATION AUTHORITY

Your health in the future

Smoking causes four times as many deaths as alcohol, drugs, traffic accidents, and all the other risks that we can try to avoid. But to many people, the risks of smoking do not seem real. When we are young, illnesses in later life may seem too far ahead to worry about. But people who did not worry when they were teenagers are today facing long illnesses. However old they are when they become ill, they will feel the same person inside as they did when they were young.

FACTS:
In the USA, about 400,000 people die each year from smoking-related diseases.
(Source: American Cancer Society)
Worldwide, 4 million people a year die from smoking-related diseases. By 2030, this figure is expected to rise to 10 million.
(Source: World Health Organization)

'Virtually every activity involves some potential risk, whether it be smoking, skiing, swimming or driving a car.'
US tobacco company *Philip Morris*

◀ *Cigarette makers sometimes compare smoking with other risky but enjoyable pastimes such as windsurfing. Yet most sports improve rather than damage our health.*

case study · case study · case study · case study · case study

Every year for twenty years, Sheila made a New Year's resolution to give up smoking, but each time she failed. She was smoking forty a day, and even when she lost her job as a shop manager, and had little money, she carried on smoking. If anything, she smoked more when she was out of a job. Often, money went on cigarettes rather than food.

Sheila and her husband felt things couldn't get much worse for them, but then Sheila found she had lung cancer. She had to have weeks of chemotherapy and radiotherapy. She lost her hair and felt tired and sick most of the time. Sheila's treatment can't cure her because the cancer has spread.

Sheila's two boys are in their teens. Some of their friends are already smokers. Sheila knows that they may start smoking because she took it up even though her own mum had died of cancer. Somehow, she felt it would never happen to her because she had always felt healthy until recently.

▲ *Cancer patients can face a long illness. They may need to take strong anti-cancer drugs, which can cause side effects, such as making their hair fall out.*

66

'A cigarette is the only freely available consumer product, which, when regularly consumed as indicated, kills.'
World Health Organization

99

The cost of the habit

If you smoke, your breath, hair and clothes may all smell of stale tobacco smoke. Tar and nicotine make your teeth look yellow or grey, and tar stains your fingers yellow. Tobacco smoke dries the skin and damages it. Even young smokers may show signs of ageing as early as their twenties. Their skin may look dull and lines may form around their mouth and eyes. Smoking can also spoil the taste of food.

▼ Smokers may age quickly. This young smoker already has wrinkles.

Smokers are less fit than non-smokers. They often become breathless when they exercise. Few successful sports people or athletes are smokers. Many smokers have coughs because their body is trying to clear the lungs. They have more health problems than non-smokers – someone who smokes twenty cigarettes a day is twice as likely to take time off work as a non-smoker.

◄ We can tell that this man is a smoker by looking at his hands. His fingers and nails are badly stained by the tar from cigarettes.

'I didn't think I smelt of smoke. I have always been really careful about cleaning my teeth properly and things like that. It really upset me when I kissed this girl and she told me my breath smelt like an ashtray!'
Josh, college student, aged 19

FACT:
From 1950 to 2000, around 62 million people died from diseases caused by smoking. That is more than all the people killed in the Second World War.
(Source: World Health Organization)

▼ *Like many regular smokers, this girl suffers from a morning cough, as her lungs try to clear themselves.*

There is no 'safe' level of smoking, and there is a health risk from all smoking, including herbal or low-tar cigarettes, cigars and pipes. Half of all the people who become long-term smokers will be killed by tobacco.

Smokers also face the huge cost of their habit. It's estimated that someone who starts smoking at the age of twenty spends around £60,000 – perhaps as much as buying their home – on cigarettes during their working life.

"

'Cigarette smoking is now as important a cause of death as were the great epidemic diseases such as typhoid, cholera and tuberculosis that affected previous generations in this country.'

The British Royal College of Physicians

5. Living and working with smokers

What is passive smoking?

Do you think it is right to ban smoking from public places? Some people think that smokers should be able to smoke wherever they want. But now we know more about the risks of passive smoking, many people believe that non-smokers have the right to clean air.

Passive smoking means breathing in someone else's cigarette smoke. When someone smokes a cigarette, they only inhale 15 per cent of the smoke. The rest goes into the air. Being in a smoky room can make some people feel dizzy and give them coughs, red eyes, sore throats, headaches and breathing problems. Scientists believe that passive smokers are 10–30 per cent more likely to get lung cancer than people who do not live or work with smokers.

> 'After I have been to work, the next morning I am coughing like a smoker. I used to think it wasn't worth quitting because working in a bar is just like smoking.'
> *Nicole, bartender and waitress*

▶ *These young women in a bar in Paris are lighting up while they have a drink. In the USA, some bars have banned smoking, but smokers' rights groups have fought against the ban.*

▶ *Cinemas used to be smoky places until no-smoking areas were introduced. Now, smoking is banned in many cinemas in Europe and the USA.*

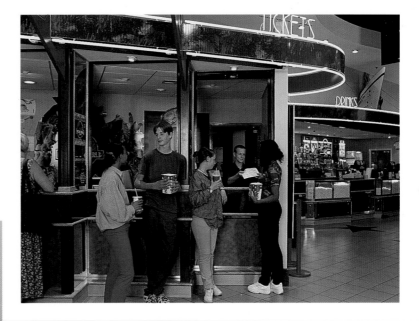

“ **'Even if smokers are in a minority, their needs should still be catered for.'**
Tobacco Manufacturers' Association ”

In Europe and the USA, smoking is now banned in many public places such as buses, cinemas and restaurants. Other places may have no-smoking areas. Many companies are bringing in no-smoking policies. They are worried they might be taken to court for failing to protect their workers from passive smoking.

FACTS:
In the USA, research has shown that around 3,800 people a year die from lung cancer caused by passive smoking.
(Source: US Environmental Protection Agency)
A recent US study found that bar and restaurant workers are one and a half times more likely to get lung cancer than the rest of the population.

Denmark has the highest rate of smoking in the European Union, and the highest rate of women smokers in the world. A law in 1996 banned smoking in all public buildings. Health projects were set up to help people to quit.

Children's health

Almost half of all children worldwide – 700 million children – live in the home of a smoker. Children who smoke, or live with smokers, are more likely to get coughs, colds and breathing problems. They have higher levels of carbon monoxide in their blood and get tired more easily. If they have asthma, smoking can make it worse.

When both parents smoke at home, a child may passively smoke the same as if they smoked 80 cigarettes a year. Even pet cats and dogs can have skin and breathing problems because they are passively smoking their owner's cigarettes.

▲ This baby in Java, Indonesia has to breathe in his father's smoke. The child of a smoker is twice as likely to smoke himself as the child of a non-smoker.

◀ If a pet lives in the home of a smoker, it can suffer health problems from passive smoking.

30

case study · case study · case study · case study · case

Carol started smoking when she was fourteen. She tried to give up when she became pregnant several years later. Although she cut down, she carried on smoking. As her family grew, she tried not to smoke around her children, especially when they had colds or infections.

Carol had heard of asthma but she didn't know much about it until the doctor said that her ten-year-old daughter, Angharad, and nine-year-old son, Liam, were both asthmatic. Carol's doctor warned her that passive smoking would make the children's breathing problems worse. Carol tried not to smoke when the children were home from school, but she still enjoyed having a cigarette when she was watching television, or after a meal. When Liam was eleven, he had a really bad asthma attack and had to be rushed to hospital. Carol knew she had to stop smoking completely, not just for her own health but for the sake of the children.

'The anti-smoking lobby won't rest until smoking is banned in every place of work, including pubs, clubs and restaurants for which smokers represent a substantial part of their business.'
Simon Clark, director of FOREST, for smokers' rights

◀ *This boy is using a spacer to inhale his asthma medicine. Breathing in other people's tobacco smoke can bring on an asthma attack.*

Smoking in pregnancy

When a pregnant woman smokes, her baby becomes a passive smoker. The chemicals from cigarettes pass into the mother's bloodstream, and then to her baby. Nicotine makes the baby's heart beat faster. The carbon monoxide means that less oxygen gets to the baby. The baby does not grow as much as it should. Pregnant women who smoke have a higher risk of losing the baby in pregnancy, or having a premature or stillborn baby.

Women who smoke when they are pregnant may have problems with their own health. They are more likely to get ill and to have to go into hospital during their pregnancy. But it can be hard for a pregnant woman to quit. Some women are worried they will put on too much weight if they stop smoking. Others feel they need cigarettes to help them through the stresses of the pregnancy.

▲ *When a woman is pregnant, it can be hard coping with everyday chores and worries. Some women turn to cigarettes, even though they know the health risks to themselves and their baby.*

◀ *A 20-week-old baby boy in the womb. He is almost fully formed – and he may already be passively smoking.*

They might be worrying about money, housing or relationships, and what will happen once the baby is born.

About two-thirds of women who smoke give up during their pregnancy. Others manage to cut down the number of cigarettes they smoke. It can mean that they inhale more deeply when they do smoke, but this is not always the case. If a woman stops smoking before she becomes pregnant, or in the early months of pregnancy, she can reduce the health risks to herself and her baby.

FACT:
A smoker's baby weighs an average 200 grams less than a non-smoker's. Smaller babies are more likely to become ill, or even die.

'I'd been a smoker for six years before I got pregnant. I'd tried giving up before, but once I knew about the baby, I stopped just like that. I think it was when they warned me about the risk of premature birth. I didn't want to take any risks with my baby.'
Debbie, aged 24 years

◀ *Women who choose not to smoke in pregnancy give their baby a head start to good health.*

6. The profits from tobacco

Why is smoking big business?

Why is growing tobacco so popular? Tobacco makes a lot of money for tobacco growers, manufacturers, shopkeepers and governments. Worldwide, the tobacco industry takes more than $275 billion a year in sales.

Tobacco is grown in about a hundred countries around the world. Often, farmers can make more money by growing tobacco rather than food. In the USA, farmers receive about 40 times more income from a hectare of tobacco than they do for a hectare of wheat. In countries like Venezuela, tobacco manufacturers provide a fixed price for farmers and help them with farming technology.

> 'Every time someone buys tobacco products, they are supporting an industry that goes for profit before people, without regard for human suffering or environmental cost.'
> *GASP Smoke-free Solutions*

International tobacco companies are among the richest companies in the world. In the USA, the profits from tobacco are higher than the profits made by the giant computer firms.

▶ *These farmers are harvesting tobacco leaves on a farm in Cuba.*

But nowadays, fewer people in developed countries are buying cigarettes. For example, in the USA, tobacco sales are falling by about 2 per cent a year. Also, some people are taking the tobacco companies to court because of diseases caused by smoking.

The tobacco companies have started to put their money into other businesses, such as food and drinks. They are also selling more cigarettes in developing countries. For example, China now consumes around 30 per cent of the world's cigarettes. Another 30 per cent are smoked in the growing markets of South America, the Middle East, Africa and Asia.

High-tar brands and cigarettes without filters have become less popular in richer countries because of health warnings. They are now being sold to developing countries.

▲ These men in a café in Cairo, Egypt are smoking a hookah together. The tobacco used in hookahs is often high in tar and nicotine.

The tobacco companies continue to make huge profits, but they make them from different parts of the world.

Cigarette advertising – making smoking look glamorous

How many cigarette brands can you name? Cigarette manufacturers spend millions of pounds every year to make people aware of their brands.

In the USA, tobacco companies spend an estimated $11 million every day advertising their products – more than the US Federal Office on Smoking and Health spends in an entire year to prevent smoking. In some countries, tobacco companies sponsor sports and other events to make people aware of their brands. They also advertise by paying film-makers to show film stars smoking their brand – this is called indirect advertising. The tobacco industry claims that it is not trying to encourage new smokers, but to persuade people who already smoke to switch brands.

> 'There is no convincing evidence that tobacco advertising causes anybody – adult or child – to start smoking.'
> *Tobacco Manufacturers' Association*

▶ *The tobacco industry likes to link smoking with fast, glamorous sports. Sports, such as motor racing, have come to rely on sponsorship money from tobacco companies.*

Advertisers think up clever ideas to make people aware of their brands. Sometimes, they do not even show the product.

Some countries, including New Zealand, Canada, Norway, Sweden and Finland, have banned all cigarette advertising. In Norway, research shows that since advertising was banned in 1975, people are smoking fewer cigarettes, and the number of children taking up smoking has halved.

In 1998, the European Union passed a law to ban all direct advertising in member states. The British tobacco industry is fighting government proposals to ban advertising and sponsorship by tobacco companies. It needs to find 330 new smokers a day to replace those who have died from diseases caused by smoking.

'The tobacco companies…make you believe that if you smoke, you're going to be sexy, attractive, successful, accepted by your peers…they project this image in every media – from daytime movies to night-time movies, magazines and even cartoons.'

Tobacco control activist, Allen Landers

The tobacco industry – who pays and who benefits?

Governments earn billions of pounds in taxes every year from the tobacco industry. In Denmark, 84 per cent of the price of a packet of cigarettes is tax. The British Government received over £10 billion in tax from the tobacco industry in 1998. But every year, billions of pounds are spent on caring for smokers who have become ill. Millions of working days are lost, too. The World Bank estimates that the world economy loses at least $200 billion a year because of the use of tobacco products.

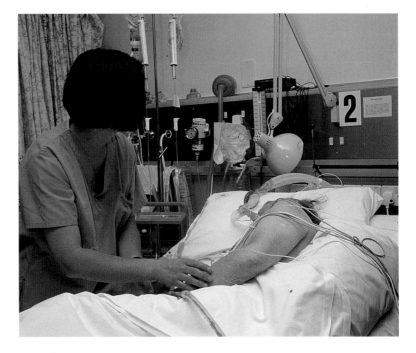

"

'The tobacco industry is a major contributor to the UK economy...[in one year] it would, for example pay for three-quarters of the Education and Employment budget or 40 Millennium Domes.'

The Tobacco Manufacturers' Association

▲ *Many smokers will end up spending a large amount of time in hospital. In the USA, medical care for tobacco-related diseases costs $50 billion each year.*

"

More companies are now becoming aware of the costs to their businesses and their workers of illnesses caused by smoking. Some have brought in rules against smoking and schemes to encourage employees to quit.

case study · case study · case study · case study · case study

Last year, Jamie was off sick from his factory on the outskirts of Glasgow for a total of thirty working days. Jamie is a heavy smoker. He has always suffered with a bad chest, and even a cold or flu can leave him unwell with a nasty cough and breathing problems for several weeks. Recently, Jamie has begun to have pains in his chest and arms. Doctors have told him he has heart trouble, made worse by his smoking habit. Jamie's employers know that his sick record is getting worse every year. They have always allowed their staff to smoke but now they are considering a no-smoking policy at work. Every year they lose hundreds of working days because of illness among their staff. A report into smoking in the workplace by the Scottish Health Education Board found that smokers take almost a third more sick leave every year than non-smokers. This costs Scottish businesses around £290 million a year.

◀ *Another day off work because of illness.*

7. Quitting the habit

How can you stop smoking?

Do you know anyone who has given up smoking? Most smokers decide at some time that they would like to give up. They may be worried about their health, or need to stop spending so much money on cigarettes.

Smokers must really want to give up if they are going to succeed. Some fail because they don't want to give up enough, or because they are only giving up to please someone else, like a partner or a doctor. Some may feel they cannot cope with life without their cigarettes. Others say they are giving up, but think it will be alright if they have a cigarette now and again.

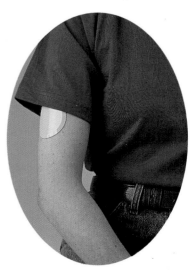

▲ Nicotine patches deliver up to 1 mg of nicotine an hour. It passes through the skin into the bloodstream to stop the craving.

◀ Chewing gum can help smokers to quit. Some people use nicotine gum, which releases a low dose of nicotine.

The first days or weeks after giving up can be hard, because the smoker's body finds it difficult to do without nicotine. During this time, people may have headaches and feel nervous and jumpy. As the level of carbon monoxide in the blood falls, more oxygen gets to the brain, so the person may start to feel dizzy, or find it hard to sleep. They feel cravings for a cigarette, especially when they are under stress or others are smoking around them.

▼ *These young people are at a group counselling session for ex-smokers. Only 1 to 3 per cent of people manage to quit without any help.*

Some smokers try using nicotine gum or patches on the skin to help them get through the first weeks. Others get help from a counsellor or join a no-smoking group, where everyone supports each other. Hypnosis and acupuncture can help some people quit.

FACTS:
54% of smokers in Britain say they want to quit.
Around 1,000 people a day do quit smoking.
(Source: QUIT)
In the USA, 70% of adult smokers say
they want to quit. 1.5 million of
them quit smoking every year.
(Source: National Centers for Disease Control
and Prevention, USA)

Quit Day

These hints can help people who want to quit:

♦ Cut down smoking gradually – or

♦ Stop on a particular day, such as New Year's Day or World No Tobacco Day, when lots of other smokers are trying to give up

♦ Keep a smoker's diary before the Quit Day. The smoker writes down when they are most likely to reach for a cigarette and thinks of other things to do instead

♦ Chew gum instead of smoking

♦ Take up exercise

♦ Eat healthy food, such as fruit, instead of smoking.

▲ Giving up smoking need not mean putting on weight. Eating a healthy diet and exercising will help an ex-smoker to keep in shape.

Some people worry that they will put on weight when they stop smoking because they will be tempted to eat more. Food certainly tastes better if you don't smoke, and ex-smokers may find that their weight increases slightly. It usually settles after a month or two.

◄ This girl is enjoying a swim. Being a non-smoker is part of living a healthy life.

case study · case study · case study · case study · case study

John is in his early forties. He started smoking when he became a lorry driver in his twenties, getting through about fifty cigarettes a day. Smoking and listening to the radio made the job a bit less boring. When he got home, John always felt too tired to exercise, until his partner Sandra bought a lurcher pup. John found himself taking the growing dog for long walks at the weekends.

It was then that John began getting bad pains in his legs. He went to the doctor, who told him that his blood had become thick and sticky. The arteries in his legs were so clogged that there was a risk that John could lose his legs, or die. John knew that his only chance was to give up smoking and get fitter. It was hard because he had always had a packet of cigarettes in his cab. John got used to smoking a dummy cigarette and used nicotine skin patches to help him over the first few weeks. With Sandra's support he stopped smoking altogether. Now when he feels like having a cigarette, he takes the dog out instead.

▶ *Getting out and about, but keeping away from places where people are likely to smoke, can make it easier to quit.*

Feeling healthy again

Smokers who give up understand the health risks and what it means to be addicted to a drug like nicotine. They know that even if they feel bad when they first give up, they will soon start to feel better.

When smokers quit, they will begin to feel fitter and less breathless when they exercise. They will smell nicer, their clothes will no longer smell of stale tobacco smoke, and their skin will look better.

'If you want to stop smoking, any method can help. If you don't want to stop, no method will help.'
The Health Education Authority

▼ *Non-smokers have more money to spend on things they enjoy; these boys saved up for their bikes.*

Ex-smokers find that their teeth and fingers gradually lose the tar stains. They feel better about themselves because they are no longer relying on a drug to get through life, and they have more money to spend on treats that are good for them.

After a few weeks, the blood circulation improves and after a few months, the lungs start to clear and work properly. Gradually, the health risks reduce. After about fifteen years, an ex-smoker has the same risk of early death as a non-smoker.

'I felt awful at first. I was told it was the body's reaction to getting rid of all that rubbish. Now I feel so much better.'
James, finalist in QUIT's awards for UK Quitter of the Year, 1999

◀ *These girls have been training for a running event. Choosing not to smoke is a lifestyle choice, like choosing to do sports or get fit.*

'You have to understand what's going on in your head…when I want a cigarette I think, "but wouldn't it be awful to go through all that again". For one cigarette it's just not worth it.'
Lauren, ex-smoker

GLOSSARY

Acupuncture
A way of treating addiction, pain or illness by pricking the skin with needles.

Addiction
When a person has a desperate need for something, such as a drug, and cannot give it up without help.

Asthma
An illness that causes breathing problems.

Bronchial
To do with the lungs.

Bronchitis
A disease that makes the air tubes in the lungs swell up.

Chain-smoker
Someone who smokes so much that they often light up a cigarette from the one they are already smoking.

Chemotherapy
The treatment of disease, especially cancer, using chemical substances.

Cravings
The strong need or desire for something.

Emphysema
A disease that damages the lungs and causes breathing problems.

Epidemic disease
A disease that spreads very widely among people in an area at a certain time.

Filter
The part at the top of most cigarettes which removes some of the poisonous chemicals so that the smoker doesn't breathe them in.

Herbal cigarettes
Cigarettes made from a mixture of herbs instead of tobacco.

Hypnosis
Putting someone into a kind of sleep in order to treat them, for example, for addiction.

Inhale
To breathe in, for example, air or tobacco smoke.

Nicotine
A chemical in cigarettes that makes smokers keep wanting to smoke.

Passive smoking
Breathing in other people's cigarette smoke.

Pesticides
Chemicals used to kill insects that are harmful to crops.

Premature
Too early; before the normal time.

Quit
To give up.

Radiotherapy
The treatment of cancer and other diseases using X-rays.

Snuff
Tobacco that is sniffed through the nose.

Sponsor
To support a sports or arts event as a way of advertising a product.

Stillborn
When a baby is born dead.

Tar
A dark, thick substance in tobacco. Different brands of cigarette have different amounts of tar, so they are labelled high-tar or low-tar.

FURTHER INFORMATION

ORGANIZATIONS

UK

ASH (Action on Smoking
and Health)
102 Clifton Street
London EC2A 4HW
Tel: 020 7739 5902
www.ash.org.uk
Campaigns for policies to
control the health problems
caused by tobacco

FOREST
Audley House
13 Palace Street
London SW1E 5HX
Tel: 020 7233 6144
www.forest-on-smoking.org.uk
Campaigns for smokers' rights

GASP Smoke-free Solutions
93 Cromwell Road
Bristol BS6 5EX
Tel/fax: 0117 942 5185
Resources on tobacco control
and smoking education

Health Development Agency
(formerly the Health Education
Authority)
Trevelyan House
30 Great Peter Street
London SW1P 2HW
Tel: 020 7222 5300
www.hea.org.uk

QUIT
Victory House
170 Tottenham Court Road
London W1P 0HA
Tel: 020 7388 5775
Smokers Quitline 0800 002200
Helps smokers quit

WDM (World Development
Movement)
25 Beehive Place
London SW9 7QR
Tel: 020 7737 6215
www.wdm.org.uk
Campaigns against tobacco use
and promotion in the
developing world

USA

ASH (Action on Smoking
and Health)
2013 H Street NW
Washington, DC 20006
http://ash.org

Americans for Nonsmoker's
Rights
2530 San Pablo Ave
Suite J, Berkeley
California 94702

Office on Smoking and Health
at Centers for Disease Control
Mail Stop K-50
4770 Buford Highway NE
Atlanta
Georgia 30341-3742

WEBSITES

www.tobacco.org
A wealth of information on
everything to do with tobacco

www.infact.org
Information on the tobacco
industry

FURTHER READING

Face the Facts: Drugs by Adrian
King (Wayland, 1997)
Learn to say no: Smoking by
Angela Royston (Heinemann,
2000)
Viewpoints: A Right to Smoke?
by Emma Haughton (Franklin
Watts, 1996)
We're talking about smoking
by Karen Bryant-Mole (Wayland,
1995)

INDEX